March to Martyrdom

Regis Martin

March to Martyrdom

Seven Letters on Sanctity from St. Ignatius of Antioch

SOPHIA INSTITUTE PRESS
Manchester, New Hampshire

Cover by LUCAS Art & Design, Jenison, MI

Cover image: *Ignatius of Antioch Being Eaten by Lions*
(Public domain: Wikimedia Commons)

Sophia Institute Press
Box 5284, Manchester, NH 03108
1-800-888-9344
www.SophiaInstitute.com

Sophia Institute Press is a registered trademark of Sophia Institute.

paperback ISBN 979-8-88911-260-0

ebook ISBN 979-8-88911-261-7

Library of Congress Control Number: 2024940864

First printing

Dedication

For Roseanne . . . With all my love.

A soul seething with the divine eros.

— St. John Chrysostom

Contents

Prologue

DURING ST. IGNATIUS OF Antioch's lifetime (died around A.D. 107), it was difficult recognizing who Christ was, much less to openly identify with Him. But to have lived under Nero's reign, an emperor well-schooled in the practice of torture, the more diabolically devised the better, or of Diocletian, the last of the emperors determined on the liquidation of Christianity, required a level of spiritual heroism far beyond the reach of most men. Only in the early fourth century, with the conversion of Constantine, who at once permitted the public profession of Christianity, would an unmolested observance of faith become widely possible. That was a most blessed event. In his powerful little book *Prayer as a Political Problem*, French Cardinal Jean Danielou argues with great eloquence that "to cleave to Christianity then called for a strength of character of which the majority of men are not capable." This book worked a sea change in my own life when I first pounced upon it years ago in Spain. But thanks to Constantine, who, moved by a special grace to rid his reign of such obstacles, Danielou continues,

> The Gospel was made accessible to the poor, that is to say, to those very people who are not numbered among the elite. The man in the street could now be a Christian. Far from distorting Christianity, this change allowed it to become more truly itself, a people.

Faith took on a certain cultural expression, therefore—a development hastened by the freedoms accorded to the Church to assist men in the practice of virtue and piety. Catholic Christendom could then come into being. Experience revealed that apart from a social order to sustain the life of the spirit, even prayer itself, which Danielou describes as "an absolutely universal human vocation," may begin to wither and die, leaving the soul gasping for breath. "For it is practically impossible," he writes, "for any but the militant Christian to persevere in a milieu which offers him no support." Thus, Danielou concludes that "there can be no mass Christianity outside Christendom."

Regardless of the circumstances we find ourselves in, each one of us is faced with a decision: to follow God or not to follow Him. All are expected to make the same gift of self to the One, who has already given Himself so completely to us. Yes, in that dark night of His Passion and death, Christ even went to Hell on our behalf because of our sins.

And if there is to be a Christendom, a culture steeped in the Blood of the Lamb, saints will first have to seed it. Only the witness of sanctity can change the world. More than ever, then, we shall need saints.

St. Ignatius is one of those saints who transformed the world and the Church. The following pages take a brief and modest look at this heroic bishop. It contains fifteen chapters: fifteen meditations on Ignatius—his life, his letters, and his times. They aim to show how the ancient beauty of Christian truth is made new for each generation.

St. Ignatius wrote his seven letters in haste. I wrote my fifteen letters slowly, after years spent reading and rereading the epistles of this great bishop and martyr. This is not a systematic study. I've ordered these reflections more or less chronologically, and I've added theological and historical context which I hope you'll find helpful. For the most part, though, I've preferred freedom to structure—or, rather, I hope the freedom itself will give the book a kind of structure. If an Eliot poem is called "free verse," this book is written in "free prose."

"Is the object of life only to live?" asks the character of Pierre de Craon in *The Tidings Brought to Mary*, a masterpiece of lyric drama by Paul Claudel, as he places the body of his dead daughter Violaine on the table. "What does it matter?" he asks:

> Will the feet of God's children be fastened to this wretched earth? It is not to live, but to die, and not to hew the cross, but to mount upon it, and to give all that we have gladly. Herein lies joy, freedom, grace, eternal youth!

What possible weight does the world possess when compared to life, is a question each of us must answer. And what is the point of having such a life if it cannot be given? For that we shall have to ask the saints, who have answered it with their lives. Let them show us the way, then, these blessed few who have given most gladly, who, having recklessly thrown away everything for the sake of Another, are truly and lastingly happy. If the only sadness, as Léon Bloy would say, is not to be a saint, then isn't it time to get started? Let us turn then to St. Ignatius to help show us the way—to joy, freedom, grace, and eternal youth.

St. Ignatius, bishop and martyr, pray for us!

March to Martyrdom

Chapter 1

If Stones Could Speak

"The amphitheater, once consecrated to triumphs, entertainments, and the impious worship of the pagan gods, is now dedicated to the sufferings of the martyrs purified from impious superstitions."

—Pope St. John Paul II, 2000, at the Colosseum

WHEN I FIRST ARRIVED in Rome in the mid-1980s accompanied by a wife and two small children, we lived just outside the city walls, along the subway tracks that would take me each day to the University of St. Thomas, the Angelicum, where I was doing doctoral studies in sacred theology. During those early morning commutes into the historic center, there was always the same spectacle waiting to be seen—this immense, looming structure standing ever before my eyes as I began the steep climb to the university. What did it mean, what possible relevance did this huge pile of stone and cement have in a world so vastly different from the one where it had first been seen, begun and completed less than a century following Christ's birth? Here was the largest amphitheater in the world, after all, and every morning it would catch my eye, riveting my attention like nothing I'd ever seen before.

Once you've seen the Colosseum, it never leaves your mind. Why is that? There is nothing particularly beautiful about it, unlike so many lovely things in Rome; and, of course, there is no roof on it. As someone once wryly said about those ancient Roman architects, that having begun like giants, they could hardly be expected to finish like jewelers. The lure of the Colosseum was never a matter of aesthetics. It was not the beauty of the thing that moves one to stand and stare. Yes, it was huge and imposing, possessed of an undeniable grandeur, certainly. But at the end of the day was it anything more than an ancient ruin, of which there are so many examples already, amid the plastic and the neon of post-modern Rome?

No, it was something else altogether that proved so fixating. Had it something to do with faith, I wonder, that catholic and apostolic Faith I'd come all the way to Rome to study? To immerse myself in the soil of a religion whose roots reach very deep, stretching far back to Rome and beyond? "Religion is the key to history," Lord Acton once said. And it is upon that history that the truth of the Gospels depend. Belloc was not wrong when he declaimed, "Europe is the faith and the faith is Europe." Leave it out of the equation and Western Civilization makes no sense. If God did not come down among us, and if there were no martyrs to testify to Christ, then it hardly matters what we think, does it? Without the note of "ineradicable positivity," quoting an expressive phrase from Joseph Ratzinger's landmark text, *Introduction to Christianity*, then there is no music to be played, no notes to be heard. And so, like the great French theologian Jean Danielou, I too would take my stand, "loving best of all that Church mud-splashed from history."

Isn't this, moreover, why we hold in pious memory the most salient truth concerning the Colosseum, that here was the setting where countless Christians gave their lives for Christ in the most excruciating of circumstances? Why be fascinated by the sight of a ruin if one cannot draw close to those ancient stones fraught with memories that quickened the faith of so many? Ah, if only the stones could speak! If memory, as the poet Pavese reminds us, "is a passion repeated," then the mere sight of that place, of all those stones now strewn about, may serve to repeat a passion, however distant the source or vicarious the sense, for what it was those men and women endured for Christ.

Have I anyone in particular in mind here, someone perhaps whose own example has long fired the imagination of the faithful? It has certainly fired mine. And I do. His name is Ignatius, the sainted bishop and martyr of Antioch, who offered his life in the Colosseum in the year A.D. 107. In this precise place where, centuries later, I'd be exiting a subway, he shed his blood for the God-Man, Jesus Christ. And trudging up the hill day after day toward the Angelicum, I resolved to learn all that I could about his life and the lives of others annealed in heroism and hope before the incarnate God.

Conversion is at the heart of Catholicism. But what does it mean to be converted? It means, to recall the wonderful description of Fr. Antonin Sertillanges, "simply meeting yourself for the purpose of going to the very end of your being." If that's what it means, then St. Ignatius of Antioch had certainly met himself long before going to the very end of his being. "Conversion means a willingness to see the truth of things and to conform one's conduct to it," said Fr. Sertillanges. To whom did

St. Ignatius conform his conduct, indeed the whole configuration of his life, if not to Christ?

He knew where he was going, and why he was going there. "When a man loses everything in life except life," writes Victor Frankl in his signature work, *Man's Search for Meaning*, "what will enable him to survive?" The cruelest deprivations of the body cannot constrain the soul so long as a higher horizon beckons it forward. Even Nietzsche understood that. "Those who have a why to live," he declared, "can bear with almost any how."

St. Ignatius had a why. And he would be the first to tell you what it was. In fact, he did tell us, and at copious and vivid length in a series of impassioned letters sent along the way from Antioch to Rome where the beasts hungrily awaited his arrival. What short work they must have made of him that blessed day at the turn of the second century!

I'd like to examine St. Ignatius's seven inspiring letters to see what ideas arise through them. Specifically, I would like to know why they were so important to Ignatius and to the early Church whose brave champion he had become; why they ought to be no less important to us as well, from whose example of life we may be edified and by whose exposition of doctrine enriched.

And while our current prospects may appear bleak and challenging, they were not so different for him, either. We've much to learn from St. Ignatius. Therefore, I'm eager to return to the beginning when, as von Balthasar would say, the Church found herself seventeen years old, full of the faith and the hope and the love of Christ. "We shall not collect the living and sacred documents of our life (and the history of the Church is our life) as a person would collect stamps or butterflies," he writes in *Presence and Thought: An Essay on the Religious Philosophy of Gregory of Nyssa*. "That would be to demonstrate that we are already dead." Von Balthasar continues:

> Let us read history, our history, as a living account of what we once were, with the double-edged consciousness that all of this has gone forever and that, in spite of everything, that period of youth and every moment of our lives remain mysteriously present at the wellsprings of our soul in a kind of delectable eternity.

This is how we'll enter into the life of St. Ignatius of Antioch. We'll begin at the beginning of the end: the road to the Colosseum.

Chapter 2

The Heroic Witness of St. Ignatius

"God is the fire my feet are held to."

—Last line of "Ars Poetica II" by Charles Wright

IT WAS NOT WITH airline or train ticket in hand that St. Ignatius arrived in Rome near the end of the first century. "A soul seething with the divine eros," is how St. John Chrysostom would describe the sainted bishop and martyr three centuries later in a homily preached on his feast day in Antioch. He did not travel first class, or even coach, on that final visit to the imperial capital. Not in this world, he didn't. As for the journey home, one can only imagine the rocket ship needed to propel him instantly into the waiting arms of God.

Despite having the highest episcopal standing in the Church at Antioch, where scarcely a half-century before the seed of faith had been planted by Paul and Barnabas,

St. Ignatius received no warm welcome in Rome. Indeed, his reception proved to be even more brutal and degrading than the trip itself, which stretched many hundreds of miles along the overland route through Asia Minor, including cities and towns so ancient that their names are no longer remembered. Cilicia? Laodicea? Magnesia? Does anyone without a Classics degree know where these places are?

No one knows how long St. Ignatius's trip took. He painfully journeyed through much of Asia Minor, then along the western coast of what is now Turkey, embarking by boat at Troas, site of the ancient city of Troy, before finally reaching Rome. All the while, of course, as befits a condemned prisoner, being shackled to a squad of Roman soldiers—"ten leopards," is how he described them. He was literally dragged from one end of the empire to the other. Not your typical pilgrimage to Rome.

So, why did he come to Rome in the first place? Was there imperial business that couldn't wait another day? There was. In fact, the emperor himself had gone to Antioch to transact it, there overseeing a swift and brutal persecution. In the course of which, St. Ignatius was arrested and shipped off to Rome where, like an animal tied to a stake, wild dogs would devour him for the delectation of the mob. The latter took place nearly on schedule, in the year A.D. 107, under the reign of Trajan, that fierce and ruthless emperor who personally signed St. Ignatius's death warrant.

A grim story, to be sure, but one mustn't be too gloomy in recounting it. That's because it all turned out exactly as St. Ignatius, along with the Holy Ghost, had scripted it. He longed for martyrdom, you see, orchestrating in advance all the details of a drama that could end only in the triumph of death. "Let me be fodder for wild beasts," he told the Church in Rome, whose members he enjoined from doing anything whatsoever to interfere with the culminating scene of his life. "That is how I can get to God," he confided. "I am God's wheat and I am being ground by the teeth of wild beasts to make a pure loaf for Christ."

It was not in defense of any sort of abstract principle that drove St. Ignatius to such an extremity as to choose death, despising even the most cruel and pitiless of its torments. He knew all that awaited him at the other end, amid the blood and the cries of the Colosseum. And yet, he did not shrink from so awful a prospect. He embraced it rather with all the eagerness of an ardent young suitor going to meet his bride. It was the love of

Christ, the Person of the God-Man, who had come to possess his very soul, that moved him to make his final gesture of complete self-giving. "To share in his Passion I go through everything," he declared. No other writer of the early Church has expressed with such passion, such blazing intensity, the desire for union with Christ, for unending life in Christ. "It is better for me," he insisted, "to die on behalf of Jesus Christ than to reign over all the ends of the earth.... Him I seek, who died for us: him I desire, who rose again for our sake.... Permit me," he will repeatedly implore the Christians of Rome, "to be an imitator of the Passion of my God!"

> Now is the moment I am beginning to be a disciple. May nothing seen or unseen begrudge me making my way to Jesus Christ. Come fire, cross, battling with wild beasts, wrenching of bones, mangling of limbs, crushing of my whole body, cruel tortures of the devil—only let me get to Jesus Christ!

Here is conviction both rare and resolute, altogether consuming even, which leaves no room for either deflections of the will, or distractions of the mind, in getting back to Christ.

No creature in Heaven, or on earth, or under the earth, will St. Ignatius suffer to come between him and Christ.

How far this is from the usual soft soap and sentimentality of those who put on faith as if it were an electric blanket or warm fuzzy. This is not the bourgeois Christianity so many of us have grown accustomed to, with its sniveling insistence on not disturbing in the least the comfort zone we've constructed to keep out God. Minimizing the demands of discipleship lest they prove too onerous to bear is not an option for Christians. For the Cross of Christ was never meant to be easy to carry. As a result, many prefer a soft Christianity where distracting pleasures shift their aim from Calvary to this passing world. God may have intended us to reach for the stars, but our trajectories are far less lofty, and do not require that we leave planet Earth where the air is always comfortable. Having so domesticated our dreams that we needn't settle for more, what we long for is the mediocrity of those who are always at their best.

"Any Christian who is not a hero," writes Léon Bloy, that great Pilgrim of the Absolute, "is a pig." St. Ignatius of Antioch was no pig. Where, then, does that leave us?

Chapter 3

On the Trail of St. Ignatius

THERE WERE ALTOGETHER SEVEN letters sent by St. Ignatius to various communities of the faithful lying between Antioch and Rome—the latter, of course, being the place of rendezvous where ravenous beasts eagerly awaited his arrival. St. Ignatius's martyrdom took place roughly seventy-four years after the King of Martyrs, Jesus Christ, shed His blood for mankind.

The first four letters were written in Smyrna, a large and bustling Greek city located along the Aegean coast, some thirty-five miles north of Ephesus, Rome's provincial capital and an important link in the trade route joining the Aegean with the East. That it had also been the setting for St. Paul's missionary initiatives, plus the later activity of St. John the Beloved, lends it a special aura. But it was in Antioch that the name *Christian* first surfaced, becoming the designated term for the followers of Jesus, one of whom, Ignatius—called Theophorus, one who is filled with God—remains the central figure in the story.

Both Ephesus and Smyrna, by the way, along with Philadelphia, were among the seven churches expressly identified by the apostle John, author of Revelation, the last of the New Testament books, written near the end of the first century. Banished by the emperor Domitian to the Isle of Patmos, he writes as an old man, no longer the youthful John whose head rested upon the breast of the Lord. "I was in the Spirit on the Lord's day," he tells us, "and I heard behind me a loud voice like a trumpet saying, 'Write what you see in a book and send it to the seven churches, to Ephesus and to Smyrna and to Pergamum and to Thyatira and to Sardis and to Philadelphia and to Laodicea'" (Rev. 1:10–11).

Could it be, then, that Ignatius knew John? Although there is no internal evidence from the correspondence itself to suggest that either one knew the other, on the authority of St. Jerome, who lived in Bethlehem two centuries later and translated the Bible from Greek to Latin, one might imagine otherwise. "John the Apostle," he records in his *Chronicon*, "survived all the way to the time of Trajan. After whom his notable disciples were Papias, Bishop of Hieropolis, Polycarp of Smyrna, and Ignatius of Antioch."

Is it not at least likely, in the circumstance, that the disciple, that is, Ignatius, might have known something of the man whose disciple he was, that is, John? All of which transpiring, let's not forget, during the reign of an emperor named Trajan, who did nothing to end the banishment of the one, nor to prevent the death of the other. In fact, he gleefully signed the warrant for his execution on a state visit to Antioch.

And then, of course, there is Eusebius, one of whose chapters in *The History of the Church* is about St. Ignatius, his life, and the letters he wrote, both of which Eusebius finds entirely credible. Does he connect the same dots? He does.

But the most telling testimony of all has got to be from St. Irenaeus, who provides the actual paper trail, tracing everything back, from St. Ignatius to St. Polycarp, through the apostle John, to the Person of Christ Himself. In other words, St. John knew St. Polycarp—having, after all, ordained him bishop of Smyrna—and since they (St. Polycarp and St. Ignatius) knew each other (indeed, one of Ignatius's letters is addressed to him), it seems entirely plausible that John and Ignatius would have known each other as well. The figures on the chessboard are not so numerous, nor the area of possible intersection so vast, that it is wholly unlikely for a few good men of holiness and learning to cross paths occasionally. God's grace can orchestrate anything, especially a meeting between saints.

Furthermore, St. Irenaeus himself, the most formative figure in the development of Western theology, did most certainly know Polycarp. After all, Irenaeus was born in Smyrna around the time when Polycarp became its bishop. And as a young man he became his student, later on moving to Lyons in southern Gaul, where he became its bishop and, not long after, its martyr.

Concerning St. Polycarp, his great mentor and teacher, St. Irenaeus, writes as follows:

> Polycarp was not only instructed by the apostles, and conversed with many who had seen Christ, but was also, by apostles in Asia, appointed bishop of the Church in Smyrna … always taught the things which he had learned from the apostles, and which the Church has handed down, and which alone are true. To these things

> all the Asiatic Churches testify, as do also those men who have succeeded Polycarp.

Let us assume, then, that what the lawyers like to call, "establishing the chain of evidence," which is to say, the physical details that connect one thing with another, appears now to be in place.

So, what is St. Ignatius, a condemned prisoner bound for execution in Rome, doing in Smyrna? Forgive the flippancy, but there was no direct flight from Antioch to Rome. Why the stopover in Smyrna? The answer is obvious. Smyrna, for all its size and its pretentions to self-importance, is nothing more than a place of respite, a halfway house, as it were, following the harsh rigors of a journey that first began in Antioch, a city far to the east. So why have they stopped? Perhaps at some point they'll need to water the horses, feed and re-provision the men, including Ignatius, whom presumably they are expected to keep alive lest the wild beasts be deprived of a meal at the other end. Yes, Rome wants Ignatius alive, for the love of entertainment.

Smyrna would not be St. Ignatius's final stop before Rome. Along the northern route, which will carry them to the edge of Asia, he would visit the port city of Troas, situated along the Aegean, the nearest possible point of entry to Europe, beyond which lies a world where reason is revered, where truth and mind are real categories. In short, where *logos*, not *mythos*, is made welcome among men. And there, amid the precincts of Europe, the receptivity of nature to grace, reason to revelation, is greater. "I am convinced," writes Joseph Ratzinger in his landmark *Introduction to Christianity*, a book so captivating that no sooner had Paul VI read it than he made him a bishop, "that at bottom it was no mere accident that the Christian message, in the period in which it was taking shape, first entered the Greek world and there merged with the enquiry into understanding, into truth."

Why else would we be told about Paul, who, in the book of Acts (16:6–10), will be forbidden by the Holy Spirit "to speak the word in Asia," and thus be prevented from going into Bithynia to preach? Unless, of course, that same Spirit had urged him elsewhere—indeed, "as a divinely arranged necessity," says Ratzinger—into the Hellenistic world, where the seed of the gospel awaits a yet greater harvest than the mythic bins of Asia can contain?

Moved thus by a strange compulsion to leave Troas and the cities and towns of Asia—the precise impetus for which being a vision in which "a man of Macedonia was standing beseeching him and saying, 'Come over to Macedonia and help us,'" Paul and his companions set sail for Europe, into that very region where the grace of God has drawn them.

And in his turn, not too long after, Ignatius will follow, bound likewise for Rome where a glorious fulfillment awaits him as well. But not before certain letters need to be sent.

Chapter 4

St. Paul and St. Ignatius: Two Witnesses to Christ

THE MOST IMPORTANT OF St. Ignatius's letters was also the longest: his epistle to the Ephesians. The Ephesians were a Christian community with whom the apostle Paul had similar dealings a half-century before. In fact, it was Paul who, in the company of Barnabas, had first evangelized the Church of Ephesus into existence, spending no little time there between the years A.D. 52 and A.D. 54. In the circumstance, therefore, perhaps a brief word about Paul and his apostolate to the Ephesians may be helpful.

It was ten years after his sojourn in Antioch, while languishing in a Roman prison, that Paul wrote his letter to the Ephesians, exhorting them to remain steadfast in their common faith, a faith rooted in God himself, who, Paul assures them, "chose us in [Christ] before the foundation of the world, that we should be holy and blameless before him" (1:4).

And because they stood redeemed by the blood of Christ, they were urged to live as though all sin and division had been wiped away by the pure sacrifice of His Cross. Without the torture of execution, and the grace and the truth imparted by Christ's Passion and death, there can be no salvation. All that is good and true, beautiful and just, therefore, depends on Christ, on the event of His coming among us. Indeed, from the first instant of the Incarnation, of the Word's insertion into the womb of the Blessed Virgin, everything changed, nothing would ever remain the same again.

This, says Paul, was the Father's intention from the very beginning, "the mystery of his will, according to his purpose which he set forth in Christ as a plan for the fulness of time, to unite all things in him, things in heaven and things on earth" (Eph. 1:9–10).

Christ is our peace, our only peace. On this point St. Paul is most wonderfully insistent, knowing that without it the ancient enmity of Jew and Gentile will not end, can never end. "[He] has made us both [Jews and Gentiles] one, and has broken down the dividing wall of hostility, by abolishing in his flesh the law of commandments and ordinances, that he might create in himself one new man in himself in place of the two, so making peace … bringing the hostility to an end" (Eph. 2:14–16).

We are not saved by a mere preacher man, but by the Son of the living God.

And thus, on a note of singular and triumphant hope, the apostle to the Gentiles will declare to the Church of Ephesus: "So then you are no longer strangers and sojourners, but you are fellow citizens with the saints and members of the household of God" (2:19). Having thus reminded them of their high destiny, St. Paul tells them:

> [You were] built upon the foundation of the apostles and prophets, Christ Jesus himself being the cornerstone, in whom the whole structure is joined together and grows into a holy Temple in the Lord; in whom you also are built into it for a dwelling place of God in the Spirit. (Eph. 2:20–22)

What stirring sentiments from St. Paul. Indeed, language so beautiful that it is no surprise that St. Paul's letter will enter the New Testament record where, from its canonical perch, it will inspire Christians everywhere. St. Ignatius? Was St. Ignatius, in writing to the same community of Christians near the end of the first century, aware of St. Paul's missive? Was he influenced by his style? Had he even heard of the great apostle to the Gentiles?

Scholarly opinion may not, even now, be entirely settled on the extent of Paul's influence (or John's, for that matter) on the life and thought of Ignatius. Certainly, the experts tell us, he knew several of Paul's letters, perhaps the whole corpus, and was especially familiar with Corinthians. But was he a close student of the Letter to the Ephesians as well and what difference does it finally make? In the perspective of Christ, it makes no difference whatsoever. Because, finally, under the aspect of the heavens, what fired the imagination and fueled the faith of all three was nothing less than God Himself, the Father of Our Lord and Savior Jesus Christ, whose Holy Spirit moved each one of them to fall wholly in love with Christ.

So, turning to St. Ignatius, the question is—What exactly is in this Letter to the Church of Ephesus, written on the fly, as it were, on his way to Rome to die? Three themes inform its telling, the first and most obvious of which being his approaching death, which he's determined to get right. "For you were all zeal to visit me when you heard that I was being shipped as a prisoner from Syria for the sake of our common Name and hope," he tells those who have come to see him in Smyrna, the setting of four of the seven letters sent by Ignatius. "I hope, indeed, by your prayers to have the good fortune to fight with wild beasts in Rome, so that by doing this I can be a real disciple."

And yet, he remains uncertain as to whether he will prove himself equal to the task set before him. "For even if I am a prisoner for the Name, I have not yet reached Christian perfection. I am only beginning to be a disciple, so I address you as my fellow students." To wear a crown of martyrdom, which St. Ignatius so ardently desires, he asks for their "coaching in faith, encouragement, endurance, and patience."

The two remaining themes will be briefly mentioned here and addressed later in more detail. The first theme involves unity. The bishops are called to keep souls in the sheepfold of the Church by virtue of their office. St. Ignatius keenly embraces this role. "I hasten to urge you to harmonize your actions with God's mind. For Jesus Christ—that life from which we cannot be torn—is the Father's mind, as the bishops too, appointed the world over, reflect the mind of Jesus Christ."

The second theme involves Christ Himself, the absolute centrality of His Person and work, which not a few heretics and schismatics have sought to subvert. "Some, indeed," St. Ignatius warns, "have a wicked and deceitful habit of flaunting the Name about, while acting in a way unworthy of God. You much avoid them like wild beasts. For they are mad dogs which bite on the sly." The language is colorful, but the fear is real, against which all the weight of Christian conviction will come into play.

Chapter 5

A Visionary Anchored to Planet Earth

And he who sat upon the throne said,
"Behold, I make all things new."

(Rev. 21:5)

THE NEW AND ETERNAL Easter is already underway, paid for by the Passion of the Son. "In the Great Sea of our Usual Life," says Luigi Giussani, referencing this sundering, transcendent event, "a Continual Newness." In the light of that profound, transformative event, how are we to view the Church? Well, it's fairly obvious, isn't it? She belongs to Him, to the very one who bought the Bride, purchasing her with His very own blood. She is not, therefore, something any of us could make, but rather Someone, a Bride, whom He alone has made, fashioned from the blood and brokenness of His body as it hung upon the Cross.

Here a line from St. Augustine practically leaps onto the page: "Mundus reconciliatus Ecclesia." "The Church is the world, reconciled." She is the setting for all that now springs eternal. "This new city," Henri de Lubac reminds us in his magnificent work *The Splendor of the Church*, "the sheltering womb and matrix of the new world, is the Church—the new universe." And quoting St. Gregory of Nyssa, he adds: "The foundation of the Church is the creation of a new universe. In her, according to the words of Isaiah, new heavens and a new earth are created; in her is formed another man, in the image of Him who created him."

And so, if that's the baseline belief of the Christian, and few have steeped themselves as thoroughly as St. Ignatius into its ecclesial depths, then let the following passage from his Letter to the Ephesians provide the most perfect summary, indeed, the most exquisite evocation of it:

> A star shone forth in the heaven above all the stars, and its light was unutterable. Its strangeness caused amazement, and all the rest of the constellations with the sun and the moon formed themselves into a chorus about the star. But the star itself outshone them all. And

> there was bewilderment whence this unique novelty had arisen. As a result all magic lost its power and all witchcraft ceased. Ignorance was done away with, and the ancient kingdom of evil was utterly destroyed, for God was revealing himself as a man, to bring newness of eternal life. What God had prepared was now beginning. Hence everything was in confusion as the destruction of death was being taken in hand.

Here is a vision that dazzles even as it describes. And if you ask on what basis so dazzling a description depends, the answer is *Incarnation*. "The hint half guessed, the gift half understood, is Incarnation," writes T. S. Eliot in *Four Quartets*. For St. Ignatius, it is neither half guessed, nor half understood. And its implication is that when God chose to become man in Palestine, He willed His grace upon all to shine. "For what Christ once in humbleness began," says the poet George Herbert, "We him in glory call, The Son of Man."

The key here is *humility*—"the only wisdom," says Eliot, "we can hope to acquire"—without which there can be no Incarnation. Nor any Redemption, either.

St. Ignatius clearly understood this. In fact, pursuant to the truth of it, he will tell the Ephesians about "three secrets crying to be told, but wrought in God's silence," which managed totally to escape "the notice of the prince of this world." And what were those secrets? "Mary's virginity and her giving birth," says St. Ignatius, followed by "the Lord's death." From womb to tomb, crib to Cross—Christ's march through the human and finite world, lifting it all onto the plane of infinite and divine glory.

This vision drives the bishop of Antioch's mind and heart, soon to become a martyr of the Church he leads and loves.

So, why should any of these secrets have escaped the notice of the Evil One? Because, clothed as they are in perfect humility, they will all the more easily confound the satanic pride of the Dark Lord, who could never foresee the coming nor, so blinded is he by pride, the inevitable conquest wrought by a God unafraid to immerse Himself in time. The unnoticed humility of God that broke the sham kingdom of Satan in two.

"The last days are here," writes St. Ignatius. "So let us abase ourselves and stand in awe of God's patience," which is an act of humility. "Either let us fear the wrath to come or let us value the grace we have: one or the other. Only let our lot be genuine life in Jesus Christ." Either the dread of something worse were we to persist in wickedness, or the delight God wishes to give when we turn to Him.

Because martyrdom is never far from his mind, indeed, it hovers constantly about, he will add:

> Do not let anything catch your eye besides him, for whom I carry around these chains—my spiritual pearls! Through them I want to rise from the dead by your prayers.

The certainty that he is moving inexorably towards his own rendezvous with death—which, for lesser men, is the event of final cancellation of all that they had hoped to achieve on their own dime—must weigh heavily upon him. It is, as I indicated early on, the first of the several themes present in the correspondence. It is there both to occupy his mind and to determine his will. This looming prospect of all that awaits him in Rome, the wild beasts in the arena especially, awakens in his heart the greatest earnest and eloquence of expression.

Chapter 6

On Obeying the Bishop

ST. IGNATIUS'S LETTERS HAVE one striking feature, that, like a thread running through the entire correspondence, stitches everything together. And that is the sense of solidarity, both profound and heartfelt, expressed by those who, at no little risk to themselves, have come to see him along the way. These souls gave comfort and encouragement to a condemned prisoner, or to receive counsel and instruction from a holy and prophetic man of God.

This is certainly the case with the Letter to the Ephesians, the first of four sent from Smyrna, a city on the coast of Asia Minor, to which a number of delegates have come to see him.

Among these are two important figures, one of whom is the bishop himself, a shy and retiring fellow (we are told) called Onesimus, who is there to represent the Church of Ephesus in its unity and love. The other is a deacon named Burrhus, who will later accompany St. Ignatius as far as Troas, acting as his secretary.

A grateful St. Ignatius receives these men, telling the Ephesians how—"In God's name, I received your large congregation in the person of Onesimus, your bishop in this world, a man whose love is beyond words. My prayer," he adds, "is that you should love him in the spirit of Jesus Christ and all be like him. Blessed is He who let you have such a bishop. You deserved it."

He is no less affirming about the deacon, Burrhus, along with several others, whom he describes in the Pauline way as "my fellow slave," an acknowledgment that, in Christ Jesus, we are all slaves, none are to be regarded as superior to any other. But Burrhus, "your godly deacon, who has been richly blessed," has especially endeared himself to Ignatius. "I very much want him to stay with me. He will thus bring honor on you and the bishop. Crocus, too," he continues, "who is a credit both to God and to you, and whom I received as a model of your love, has altogether raised my spirits (May the Father of Jesus Christ grant him a similar comfort!), as did Onesimus, Burrhus, Euplus, and Fronto. In them I saw and loved you all. May I always be glad about you, that is, if I deserve to be!"

Who are these men, whose names are lost to us, along with so many other godly souls known only to God? Where have they gone and how might we reach them? They have all gone over into the great silence of God, their voices joined to the blessed Communion of Saints.

"And what the dead had no speech for," explains T. S. Eliot in *Four Quartets*, "when living, They can tell you being dead: the communication / Of the dead is tongued with fire beyond the language of the living."

So, yes, they have all gone home to God, to share in His blessed life, and thus they are like Him in glory. But in the world of the early second century, in a place called Smyrna, where exactly are they? They are with Ignatius, a fellow Christian, a kindred soul, who very much needs their support in this time of acute and protracted struggle. The diabolical forces are not only harnessed to the machinery of the imperial state arrayed against him, but such powers and principalities have also been joined against the human race from the very beginning.

And the threat posed by the fallen angels is yet greater than any mischief Trajan may do. These brave souls' warmth and witness to Ignatius, in the midst of his enemies, must have fortified the bishop's faith and must have been especially fortifying for Ignatius to have. If we do not go to God alone, why should we have to suffer alone? Solidarity is all.

In thus extolling the company of godly men, without whom no real kinship in Christ is possible, Ignatius sounds the great theme of unity, especially around the person of the bishop, the visible sign of God's presence and power in this world. "United thus in your submission," he assures them, "and subject to the bishop and the presbytery, you will be real saints."

Love is what matters most. A free movement of the will, urged on by a mind that knows it has been redeemed, to fall completely in love with God, who bears a unique and unrepeatable Name, Jesus the Christ. And while Ignatius will not issue orders as if he were himself God, wrapping himself up, as it were, in the divine *Pleroma* itself, he is nevertheless very sure of his standing as bishop, of the authority he exercises when speaking the Name. Yet, despite his ecclesiastical rank, Ignatius believes himself unworthy of the Name: "For even if I am a prisoner for the Name, I have not yet reached Christian perfection. I am only beginning to be a disciple, so I address you as my fellow students," in constant need therefore of "coaching in faith, encouragement, endurance, and patience."

Apostasy as an option, in other words, is always on the table. And who can doubt but that in circumstances of extreme duress, even the most heroic among us may be tempted to betray Christ. Still, Ignatius hangs tough, exhorting the Ephesians to remain resolute as well, "harmonizing your actions with God's mind. For Jesus Christ—that life from which we cannot be torn—is the Father's mind, as the bishops too, appointed the world over, reflect the mind of Jesus Christ."

In other words, they are to remain always in perfect sync with the mind of the bishop. As indeed they are, says Ignatius. "Your presbytery," he tells them, "which deserves its name and is a credit to God, is as closely tied to the bishop as the strings of a harp. Wherefore your accord and harmonious love is a hymn to Jesus Christ. Yes, one and all, you should form yourselves into a choir, so that, in perfect harmony and taking your pitch from God, you may sing in unison and with one voice to the Father through Jesus Christ."

A lovely image, yes, and redolent of his musical style. But fragile, too, which is why it matters that the music be played inside the church, where the orchestration is pitch perfect owing to the bishop holding the baton. "Make no mistake about it," he warns. "If anyone is not inside the sanctuary, he lacks God's bread. And if the prayer of one or two has great avail, how much more that of the bishop and the total Church. He who fails to join in your worship shows his arrogance by the very fact of becoming a schismatic." Which is why he adds, quoting the book of Proverbs, "God resists the proud" (see 3:34).

"Let us then," he concludes, "heartily avoid resisting the bishop so that we may be subject to God."

Chapter 7

Missive to Magnesia

❧

WHILE NO RECORD EXISTS regarding how longed he stayed in Smyrna, nor a word about his living arrangements, St. Ignatius was there for a reason. Owing to his status as a condemned criminal bound for execution in Rome, he was stuck there because, quite simply, the emperor Trajan signed his death warrant in Antioch, where he had been bishop for years and years. As a result, Ignatius was shipped off to the capital by way of Smyrna. And the charge? Refusing to worship the household gods, which is a capital offense and, given his high episcopal profile, punishable by death in Rome's Colosseum. The wild beasts will soon enough be tearing him to shreds, but the journey thereto takes time and so he and the detachment of soldiers to which he is chained ("ten leopards," he calls them, "who only get worse the better you treat them"), will need to stop somewhere. So why not a coastal town along the northern route that leads most easily to Rome?

This will explain, by the way, why four of the letters written by Ignatius are postmarked, as it were, from Smyrna. First the Ephesians, followed by the Magnesians, the Trallians, and then, finally, the Romans. We've looked at the first, so it's time to move on to the next, which is Ignatius's Letter to the Church at Magnesia, a town south of Smyrna and about fifteen miles from Ephesus.

First, a word or two first about the town itself. What is this place and why is it called Magnesia? This is a serious study of a saint, mind you, so one should not be frivolous, but has it got anything to do with Milk of Magnesia? It does, actually, that being the word for a certain iron ore discovered in the area by the Greeks, the "magnetic" properties of which attract other elements of iron. From all that iron a certain magnesium hydroxide solution may be derived for use as an antacid and laxative. There you have it.

As for Magnesia itself, it is very ancient indeed, the Greeks having founded it some twenty-four centuries ago, filling it with temples to its various gods, including Zeus and Artemis, along with a stadium or two where festivals and games took place in honor of these domestic deities, on whose continued protection the various cities of the empire depended.

Like all the gods of the ancient world, they will not last, their expiration dates having been determined from all eternity by Christ's coming, and the transformations wrought by His renewal of all things human. "The temples of the gods," says Christopher Dawson, "are the most enduring works of man." But these will not endure. They and the whole pagan universe built upon their worship will, like the great god Pan himself, be forced to flee, leaving Christianity to preside over all that is left.

The world of classical antiquity is about to be baptized by the blood of Jesus Christ. Not all at once, of course, which accounts for the length, and ferocity, of the pagan refusal to bend the knee to the one true God, Lord of history and Savior of the world. But it cannot persist in idolatry forever. In the meantime, it is responsible for the predicament in which men like St. Ignatius find themselves.

So, he sends this letter to the fledging community of Christians living in Magnesia, some of whom, including their bishop, have come to greet him in Smyrna. Where, not long before, a similar delegation from Ephesus had arrived to pay their respects. He is a young bishop named

Damas, whom Ignatius greets with genuine delight and esteem ("He's a credit to God!" he exclaims), along with others all equally impressive. "You ought to respect him," he reminds the Magnesians, "as fully as you respect the authority of God." In doing so, he adds, "it is to the Father of Jesus Christ, who is everybody's bishop," whom you are really paying deference and homage.

Everything returns to the question of identity: knowing who we are—where we begin, where do we leave off—and acting on the things we know:

> We have not only to be called Christians, but to *be* Christians. It is the same thing as calling a man a bishop and then doing everything in disregard of him.

Accordingly, two sundering choices stand before us, and now that we know "everything is coming to an end, and we stand before this choice—death or life—and everyone will go 'to his own place'" (Acts 1:25), we must live resolutely on the side of life, of God and the Son whom He sent among us to die. "Run off—all of you—to one temple of God," he tells them; "to one altar, to one Jesus Christ, who came forth from one Father, while still remaining one with him, and returned to him."

What an impassioned appeal, straight from Ignatius's heart, imploring the good Christians of Magnesia not "to be led astray by wrong views or by outmoded tales that count for nothing. For if we still go on observing Judaism," and here the polemic intensifies in such a way that, for some, the characterization that follows may prove too painful for ears stuffed with ecumenical wax to hear. The bishop declares, "We admit we never received grace. The divine prophets themselves lived Christ Jesus' way." Isn't that why they faced persecution, because they were so convicted by grace that they needed to proclaim Christ to the world? "How, then, can we live without him when even the prophets, who were his disciples by the Spirit, awaited him as their teacher?"

There is the warhead, it seems to me, and one must choose: Will it be Judaism or Jesus? Ignatius does not hesitate for a moment in making his choice, and thus mounting his argument against the Judaizing efforts of some, presses on to the inexorable conclusion:

> Get rid of the bad yeast—it has grown stale
> and sour—and be changed into new yeast,

> that is, into Jesus Christ. Be salted in him, so that none of you go bad, for your smell will give you away. It is monstrous to talk Jesus Christ and to live like a Jew.
>
> For Christianity did not believe in Judaism, but Judaism in Christianity.

A perfect bullseye, I'd say.

Chapter 8

Ignatius and Polybius

Of the seven letters of St. Ignatius written in his final weeks, the shortest is the one sent to the Christians living in Tralles, a town less than twenty miles from Magnesia. But for all its brevity, there is no shortage of wit in it. Having dispatched a couple of letters already (to Ephesus and Magnesia), Ignatius has honed his craft sufficiently to make every word count. And what was it that precisely needed saying? Was there an important message that Ignatius must distill in less than a thousand words?

Suppose we begin with the bishop, a man by the name of Polybius, for whom Ignatius evinces the greatest esteem. For it is he, who, however unwittingly, will prove to be the pivotal figure in what follows:

> By God's will and that of Jesus Christ, he came to me in Smyrna, and so heartily congratulated me on being a prisoner for Jesus Christ that in him I saw your whole congregation. I welcomed, then, your godly good will, which reached me by him, and I gave thanks that I found you, as I heard, to be following God.

Ignatius was now ready for his ascent to Mt. Calvary. But it came at a price: the Office of Unity on which everything in the life of the Church depends. Where do we find that point of unity? In the person of the bishop, who occupies a seat of governance no less authoritative than that of God Himself. It is, you see, in the very accent of Jesus Christ that he, the bishop, speaks. And must thereupon be listened to.

Sadly, some bishops lust after power and always want more. They are wolves in sheep's clothing, usurpers who will receive no recompense from God. So, it is not self-aggrandizement that should possess such men, but the pure love of God and neighbor, pursuant to a common faith which it is their privilege and responsibility to uphold. Without the Office of Unity embodied and sustained by the bishop, there can be no holiness among the people whom God has charged the bishop to defend and protect. And they, of course, must submit to him. "For when you obey the bishop as if he were Jesus Christ," says Ignatius,

> you are (as I see it) living not in a merely human fashion but Jesus Christ's way, who for our sakes suffered death that you might believe in his death and so escape dying yourselves. It is essential, therefore, to act in no way without the bishop, just as you are doing. Rather submit even to the presbytery as to the apostles of Jesus Christ. He is our Hope, and if we live in union with him now, we shall gain eternal life.

Every road to eternal life must go through Christ, who is the only way to the Father and He is no roundabout way. But Christ does not wish to save us apart from His Bride, who is the Church, she who is both *mater et magister* (mother and teacher) and in whose very Office of Unity we find the bishop. Whose principal and defining work is, once again, to defend the Faith, and those who depend on that sacred deposit of faith in order to reach Heaven.

Ignatius further adds that we ought to "show the deacons respect. They represent Jesus Christ, just as the bishop has the role of the Father, and the presbyters are like God's council and an apostolic band. You cannot have a church without these. I am sure that you agree with me."

And they do, of course, owing to so strong and faithful a bishop. "In your bishop," says Ignatius, speaking confidingly to the holy people of Tralles, "I received the very model of your love, and I have him with me. His very bearing is a great lesson, while his gentleness is most forceful. I imagine even the godless respect him."

It is never possible, the saints tell us, to undertake anything of great or lasting importance in the spiritual life by human means alone. "The merely human," warns Chesterton, "will become inhuman." Does the Church imagine that she can defend the sacred deposit, and the souls who depend upon it for spiritual sustenance, by appeals to the temporal power? Not even the best can rescue a world lost in idolatry and sin. Besides which, as St. Gregory of Nyssa so shrewdly noted, "If all things were within our grasp, the higher power would not be beyond us."

The renewal of the human heart, therefore, can never be determined by those who stand in most need of it. To think otherwise is to reenact what Cardinal Robert Sarah has rightly called "the mystery of Judas," named after the one who betrayed Christ because he would not, all at once, bring the Kingdom of God to planet Earth. "First sanctity," he tells us, "then structures. If your bishop is not a saint, then become one yourself."

Fortunately for the Church, Ignatius was a saint. Only he did not know it, which is a sign of his sanctity. "God has granted me many an inspiration," he concedes — constrained by the truth to speak the truth — "but I keep my limits, lest boasting should be my undoing."

> For what I need most at this point is to be on my guard and not heed flatterers. Those who tell me ... they are my scourge. To be sure, I am ever so eager to be a martyr, but I do not know if I deserve to be. Many people have no notion of my impetuous ambition. Yet it is all the more a struggle for me. What I need is gentleness by which the prince of this world is overthrown.

What he needs, to be sure, is the example of such gentleness as he found in the mild and holy bishop who has come to be with him amid the fearfulness surrounding him. Along with the love and the prayers of the good people who make up "the holy church at Tralles in Asia."

> By God's mercy I need your love if I am going to deserve the fate I long for, and not prove a castaway.

The letter closes with great poignance and simplicity, with which Ignatius appeals both to God and to the church for that solace and strength he will need for future trials:

> My life is given for you, not only now but especially when I shall get to God. I am still in danger. But the Father is faithful: he will answer my prayer and yours because of Jesus Christ. Under his influence may you prove to be spotless.

Chapter 9

Fearless in the Face of Heresy

ALONG WITH ST. IGNATIUS'S usual repeated exhortations regarding submission to the bishop on matters of faith, and supplications to God for his impending martyrdom, a third item cannot be ignored. Even in as short a missive as the Letter to the Trallians, it screams for attention. Were one to leave it out, or even to marginalize its importance, the purpose of the correspondence would fall apart. And that is the matter of heresy, a most wicked and unwelcome thing, which the Church has always seen as a scourge of the soul, fraught with the gravest possible peril to the life of faith. Indeed, from its poisonous fallout Christianity stands in greater danger than even that which the most brutal of imperial persecutions have sought to inflict. For all the outward hostility of the pagan world, it is as nothing compared to the threat from within.

Ignatius knows all this, of course, which is why the least of his torments on the journey to Rome are the "ten leopards" dragging him across much of Asia Minor. It is the fear of heresy that bedevils him more than anything else. There is no threat greater, nor more insidious, than that posed by heresy, which amounts to a rejection of this or that distinctively Catholic belief. And what is heresy? It is any opinion adjudged to be at variance with, or held at sword's point to, the official teaching authorized by the Church herself. This is especially the case when such opinion tends to separate and divide one from the main body of believers. As the word itself suggests, heresy is what happens when one is free to pick and choose those beliefs with which one feels most at home, thus refusing all the rest. "Murdering to dissect," is how the poet Wordsworth put it, resulting in a rage of reductionism which leaves everything in ruins.

"I urge you, therefore," writes Ignatius to the Christians living in Tralles,

> not I, but Jesus Christ's love — use only Christian food. Keep off foreign fare, by which I mean heresy. For those people mingle Jesus Christ with their teachings just to gain your

> confidence under false pretenses. It is as if they were giving a deadly poison mixed with honey and wine, with the result that the unsuspecting victim gladly accepts it and drinks down death with fatal pleasure.

Christians must be vigilant, resolute, and unfailing in their resistance to the siren sound of the syncretist, that is, one who joins disparate elements that simply cannot be reconciled with the faith and the hope and the love of Jesus Christ. "Be deaf, then," he continues,

> to any talk that ignores Jesus Christ, of David's lineage, of Mary; who was really born, ate, and drank; was really persecuted under Pontius Pilate; was really crucified and died, in the sight of heaven and earth and the underworld. He was really raised from the dead, for his Father raised him, just as his Father will raise us, who believe in him, through Christ Jesus, apart from whom we have no genuine life.

Is Ignatius thinking about a particular heresy? Or is this just a scattergun approach to the problem? If you study that passage further, you'll see a certain compact—even credal—character, not unlike, say, the Creed of Nicaea that the Church will hammer out in the next century, summarizing the basic beliefs of her Faith. At the center of which stands the Incarnation of God, His very enfleshment in the human being Jesus. Not an idea or supposition about God, mind you, some shadowy abstraction wholly prescinded from the world of sensate experience. God is not this Mysterious Other, emitting epiphany rays which only the wise and the clever possess the mental acuity to identify, plucking them up like so many pieces of celestial lint for the deserving few. There is no concept of God at work here, no mental construct or conceit, to which only the brainy and the bright need apply.

The Incarnation of God is a *fact*, a datum as simple and plain as a potato. In other words, the Eternal Word Himself, the second Person of the Blessed Trinity, entered into time to become one of us. The Glory of the Lord descended into the grit, into the very depths of this most humble and realistic earth, to establish a relation to the whole human and material order, while remaining at once both immanent and transcendent to it.

To deny this—to pretend that it never happened, or that it could never happen—is the essence of heresy, of the Gnostic spirit specifically, of which there is no taint whatsoever in the mind of Ignatius. It has been the perennial human temptation, antedating Christianity, and Ignatius is the sworn enemy of all its lies and deceits. For it holds a dagger at the heart of the Catholic Thing, which insists that matter is good because God created it. And to show His love, Christ undertook the most daring descent of all into the very muck and the mire of our material world in order, not merely to lay hold of it in His own body, but to lay it all at the feet of his Father's glory.

St. Ignatius says:

> And if, as some atheists (I mean unbelievers) say, his suffering was a sham (it's really they who are a sham!), why, then, am I a prisoner? Why do I want to fight with wild beasts? In that case I shall die to no purpose. Yes, and I am maligning the Lord too!
>
> Flee, then, these wicked offshoots which produce deadly fruit. If a man taste it, he dies outright. They are none of the Father's planting. For if they had been, they would have shown themselves as branches of the cross,

> and borne immortal fruit. It is through the cross, by his suffering, that he summons you who are his members.

Even while on his way to a martyr's death, Ignatius is not above a pun or two. For Christ's enemies with whom he bravely jousts are aptly named Docetists—from the Greek word *dokeo*, meaning "seem," who, having fabricated a phony Christ—one who only "seems" to be human—prove themselves to be equally so.

Chapter 10

Segue to Sanctity

IF THE OFFICE OF Unity, symbolized by a sitting bishop, is necessary to the maintenance of faith — such has been the consuming preoccupation of St. Ignatius — holiness of life is the reason for it. And what is holiness? Nothing less than doing God's will from moment to moment, to the very last breath — an oblation of self so totalizing as to leave nothing left save God and everything else in relation to God.

Holiness changes everything. The moment "it appears on the scene," as Hans Urs von Balthasar has noted in *Razing the Bastions*, "anxiety and wrangling fall silent." How does St. Paul put it? "Have no anxiety about anything," he advises the Philippians (4:6). Fear nothing but God, in other words, for He has overcome the world. "Thus," continues von Balthasar, "one can fight against holiness, one can forbid it a certain external activity, but one cannot refute it." By all means, then, let the world have its way. Let it slap us around, frog-march us along the road to martyrdom—it matters not a whit in the final scheme of things. Because, in the end, God always has His way. As the poet W. H. Auden so aptly put it, "Legislation is helpless against the wild prayer of longing."

It is holiness alone that constitutes the most immediate and compelling sign of the Church's life, "the best proof that the Church still has something, indeed, everything, to say to the present and the coming time, *despite* her age and her wisdom of old age." The Church herself must be holy in order to generate sanctity in others. And so, while the Church herself cannot abrogate so essential an exercise of her authority—that is to say, Unity of Office—without betraying Christ Himself, who entrusted His mission to twelve mortal men and their successors, the only reason for it is to raise up saints to give glory to God.

The principal work of the Church, then, is to produce blessedness among her members.

And how in the name of Heaven can that happen if the Church has no authority to absolve sinners of all that stands in the way of their becoming saints? Without the grace of God coursing through the Sacraments, of which the Church remains the chief conduit, how are Christians expected to grow in holiness?

For the Church to be holy, catholic, and apostolic, she must be one. The sequence is not an accidental one, by the way. Because, from the very beginning—an hour or so, say, following Pentecost—she established her Articles of Faith, rooted in the four marks of the Church (one, holy, catholic, and apostolic). All the great confessional paradigms were predicated the same way: unity followed by the other three. "If one asks whether the Office is present in the Creed," von Balthasar reminds us in *A Short Primer for Unsettled Laymen*, "the answer is: certainly, above all in '*unam*' which stands before '*sanctam, catholicam*' and finally '*apostolicam ecclesiam*.' "

And unity is not some vague pious thought, either. Christ took on our flesh including all of our senses, rather than enshrine some of His ideals apart from our humanity. The Church is no mere spiritual affair, lacking material configuration. She is not a species of idealism, for which only those too fastidious for the flesh need apply. "If you do this," warns Henri de Lubac in *The Splendor of the Church*, his masterwork of ecclesiology, "then you are giving a dream the status of an extra-mental entity and trying to separate what God has united. You are not only opening the door to general doctrinal anarchy ... you are shutting out all understanding of the eternal purpose which God made in Christ Jesus our Lord." The Church is not a Platonist assembly, whose ideal appeals to the most rarefied of souls. "From the very morrow of Christ's death, a Church was in existence and living, just as Christ had constituted her."

Thus, the Church—as represented by Ignatius and countless kindred spirits like him—is no mere longing of the heart. She is not made of gossamer, nor is she the result of daydreaming, never mind the disinterested purity of their pursuit. "And if anyone," continues de Lubac, "can extract a clear-cut meaning from the terms 'apostolicity of the spirit'—as opposed to the sheer fact of historic succession—he is welcome to do so. The matter has, in any case, never been viewed thus, from the very first" he continues:

> And it seems preferable by far to believe St. Irenaeus when he depicts the Apostles as entrusting to bishops the Churches which were entrusted to themselves. If the Church today is not the apostolic Church she is not really carrying on Christ's mission and is not His Church.

The Office of Unity needs to become concrete; it must be flesh and blood, in order both to be seen and heard among all whom Christ wishes to call to Himself. Full of existential import, you might say. Von Balthasar notes the following:

> The Church could never be "one" if a visible principle of unity were not instituted in her, for we sinners always tend toward separation and sectarianism. And only what is united in this way can be catholic, i.e., all-encompassing, whereas our personal horizon can see and live only a part. Therefore, an objective sanctity must belong to this principle of unity that is the apostolic constitution of the Church—the college of Twelve with Peter as the unifying center—corresponding to its being instituted by Christ and accompanied by him.

The objective holiness inherent in the Church herself, that sheer scaffolding of sanctity upon which our lives depend, exists but for one reason, and that is to enable us, Christ's Mystical Body, to grow in holiness. The ladders exist for us to climb, to mount our individual ascent to God.

And the bottom line? What is the implication? It is clear:

> If Christians are to love and seek unity above all else, then they must permit the ecclesial principle, whose office it is to maintain this unity, to carry out its office. An anti-Roman sentiment ... is most deeply anti-Catholic. For its purpose is to pursue some imaginary unity by bypassing the office that has been instituted by Christ and is responsible for this unity.

And then, and only then, may true sanctity flourish. Returning to Ignatius—the soon to be martyred bishop of Antioch—whose fourth and final letter sent from Smyrna, destined for the community of Christians living in Rome, the appointed place where it all ends, overflows with sanctity.

We shall have a look at it in the following chapter.

Chapter 11

Rendezvous in Rome

OF ST. IGNATIUS'S SEVEN letters, the most intimate and impassioned is the one written and dispatched to the Church of Rome herself. It is an intensely personal account, saying little about either shoring up the Office of Unity, or unmasking the heretics, themes which dominate his six other letters. Instead, Ignatius focuses solely on eagerly embracing his impending martyrdom:

> Let me be fodder for wild beasts—that is how I can get to God. I am God's wheat and I am being ground by the teeth of wild beasts to make a pure loaf for Christ.... Then I shall be a real disciple of Jesus Christ when the world sees my body no more. Pray Christ for me that by these means I may become God's sacrifice.

What are we to make of this? How is one expected to respond to language so lurid, so unsettling, so strangely liturgical? With horror and revulsion? Clearly, Ignatius manifests his excessive zeal, a spiritual psychosis that is alien to the modern mind and sensibility. Had we been there to advise this poor deluded creature back in the early second century, would we not have suggested, say, extensive therapy for a soul so obviously unwell? A pharmacological solution, perhaps, to his problems?

And, of course, we'd have been flat-out wrong, having utterly and hilariously missed the mark.

Ignatius's above words about desiring to be fed to wild beasts likely made some think he was unbalanced during his life and even now. Under the aspect of the heavens—having vouchsafed us an order of grace within which nature and history are themselves nestled—nothing could be healthier, more normal, than the attitude taken by this saintly man. Pursuant to God and His holy will, he is behaving exactly as the baptismal script prescribes for every honest Christian:

> Unless a grain of wheat falls into the earth and dies, it remains alone; but if it dies, it bears much fruit. (John 12:24)

What else is martyrdom but an outward expression of an inward reality implicit in the act of becoming a Christian? Isn't this, after all, the meaning of Baptism, embedded in the very logic of the rite itself? Christian Initiation is an absolutely necessary and indispensable putting on of Christ, of dying in Christ, in order to rise with Christ. For "whoever loses his life for my sake," says Christ in all three Synoptic Gospels, "will find it" (Matt. 16:25; see Mark 8:34–35 and Luke 17:33).

The sheer certainty of persecution, therefore, followed by martyrdom, as von Balthasar reminds us in *The Moment of Christian Witness*, "constitutes the normal condition of the Church in her relation to the world, and martyrdom is the normal condition of the professed Christian." We cannot blame Ignatius if we refuse to conform to Christ, disdaining the cruciform shape His own life assumed.

Of course, every Christian will not be expected to die a martyr's death. Vatican II is very clear on this. "From the earliest times," we are told in *Lumen Gentium*, "some Christians have been called upon—and some will always be called upon—to give this supreme testimony of love to all men, but especially to persecutors. The Church therefore considers martyrdom as an exceptional gift and as the highest proof of love." And while the numbers may be few, nevertheless, "all must be prepared to confess Christ before men and follow him along the way of the cross through the persecutions which the Church will never fail to suffer."

Christ plainly told us to expect no other fate than the one He Himself faced, and so we are obliged to view our entire lives in relation to His own bloody end. "Martyrdom provides," says von Balthasar, "a horizon for the Christian life as such." Not an ideal we yearn someday to reach, but rather a reality in which, by virtue of our Baptism, we are already immersed. Christian heroism presses forward even when things remain unsettled. "In the New Testament," he explains, "the heroic element disappears, since man no longer needs to advance toward this extreme point, but is seen rather as originating from a point that Christ has already reached." Although, under the old dispensation, the heroism of the martyr "illustrates how strong the faith of a Jew ought to be, martyrdom in the New Testament reveals that such a faith, founded on the crucifixion of Christ and imparted by grace to his followers, is already real and existent."

> And he died for all, that those who live might live no longer for themselves but for him who for their sake died and was raised. (2 Cor. 5:15)

If God wishes, moreover, to see His Son reflected in the lives of men and women strengthened to Him in hope, why should it be regarded as unusual, or even unseemly, for Christians to be asked to suffer and die in His Name? For instance, Ignatius predicts that he will be a prisoner for Christ Jesus, the One whom he loves above all. "Things are off to a good start," he ventures to tell them.

> May I have the good fortune to meet my fate without interference! Grant me no more than to be a sacrifice for God while there is an altar at hand. Then you can form yourselves into a choir and sing praises to the Father in Jesus Christ that God gave the bishop of Syria the privilege of reaching the sun's setting when he summoned him from its rising. It is a grand thing for my life to set on the world, and for me to be on my way to God, so that I may rise in his presence.

What moves Ignatius to make so grand a gesture, the thing that determines his final path? It is nothing other than love of the divine Eros. "Of all possible virtuous acts," declares St. Thomas Aquinas in the *Summa*, "blood witness is the greatest proof of the perfection of love." And, yes, while it often happens that men will die for this or that cause, a Christian martyr is different, most strikingly so. "To die for love of the one who died for me in divine darkness," writes von Balthasar, consists of a "face-to-face encounter that is one of a kind, and it characterizes the uniqueness of Christian truth and existence."

To choose martyrdom, therefore, involves bearing witness to the One who bore witness to me in the dark night of an unspeakable death.

> Every source of grace—faith, love, and hope—springs from this night. Everything that I am … I am soley by virtue of Christ's death, which opens up to me the possibility of fulfillment in God. I blossom on the grave of God who died for me. I sink my roots deep into the nourishing soil of his flesh and blood.

Chapter 12

Why Martyrdom Matters

CURRENT SCHOLARSHIP REMAINS UNCLEAR as to whether St. Ignatius had visited Rome prior to his martyrdom. Certainly, Ignatius displayed a great love and esteem for the city. Not the pagan side of the place, of course, that being the reason for his martyrdom, but the Church of Rome, for whom he felt profound, even mystic devotion. Knowing that here was the place where, by God's design, foundations were laid, that the Petrine Office began—that the blood of Peter and Paul and countless others annealed in Christ had been shed—stoked his imagination like no other place on the planet.

Such examples would have helped steel his nerve for the coming crisis as well.

Plus, the current Roman state seemed worthy of admiration. His Letter to the Romans, therefore, is replete with references that testify unmistakably, effusively even, to a community of believers who appear blameless. "You are a credit to God," he tells them in the very first paragraph: "You deserve your renown and are to be congratulated. You deserve praise and success and are privileged to be without blemish." And citing a reputation widely renowned for numerous acts of charity, he reminds them:

> Yes, you rank first in love, being true to Christ's law and stamped with the Father's name. To you, then, sincerest greetings in Jesus Christ, our God, for you cleave to his every commandment—observing not only their letter but their spirit—being permanently filled with God's grace and purged of every stain alien to it.

Ignatius proceeds to answer the most burning question of all: Why has he come to Rome? Here, for Ignatius, is the heart of the matter, the central and pivotal point upon which everything else turns. "The still point of the turning world," the poet Eliot has called it. The place of intersection where time and the timeless, history and mystery, come together.

"Except for the point, the still point, / There would be no dance, and there is only the dance." Here is where all the lines are fated to converge. And not just in the life of Ignatius, but in the life of Everyman.

Von Balthasar wrote in a splendid little essay called "Martyrdom and Mission," found in a collection called *New Elucidations*, "the true and decisive motive of Christian martyrdom, which today as ever distinguishes it from every other self-offering, however heroic." It is simply a matter of giving witness, of giving testimony in one's own blood, to an event absolutely singular and unrepeatable; an event concerning which, not since St. Paul, have we seen so perfect an expression as the following:

> I have been crucified with Christ; it is no longer I who live, but Christ who lives in me; and the life I now live in the flesh I live by faith in the Son of God, who loved me and gave himself for me. (Gal. 2:20)

Nevertheless, Ignatius had another important reason for writing to the good Christians of Rome. He will urge them most vehemently to abstain from a certain activity. "Since God has answered my prayer to see you godly people," he declares, "I have gone on to ask for more." And the more, of course, is that nothing be done, that no one stand in the way of his divine destiny. Which is, quite simply, to suffer and die in the Colosseum. For Christ, that is, who (again) is his sole reason for being there. That being the case, then, "it is as a prisoner for Christ Jesus that I hope to greet you, if indeed it be God's will that I should deserve to meet my end." But only, of course, if they do not interfere, if nothing be done to interrupt the show, the drama—the divine dance—which from all eternity God wishes to see his servant Ignatius perform.

So, if it is death that Ignatius desires, does he fear anything? How about being torn to pieces, does that not give him pause? Not if we are to believe his own testimony, which is set down plainly. "What I fear," Ignatius tells the members of the Church in Rome, "is your generosity which may prove detrimental to me. For you can easily do what you want to, whereas it is hard for me to get to God unless you let me alone."

Once again, therefore, they are solemnly enjoined not to come between him and his divine destiny. If the Roman Christians wish to ingratiate themselves with the saintly bishop of Antioch, who is both a prisoner of

Christ and the empire, they must hasten to remove all possible impediments that prevent him from fulfilling God's will. However much they may be moved to action, to seize the initiative to set Ignatius free, they must not give in, they must resist doing anything. "For if you quietly let me alone," he explains, "people will see in me God's Word. But if you are enamored of my mere body, I shall, on the contrary, be a meaningless noise."

Only by becoming "fodder for wild beasts" can Ignatius prove himself worthy of the Lord, and so eligible at last to enter the Precincts of Eternal Felicity.

> What a thrill I shall have from the wild beasts that are ready for me! I hope they will make short work of me. I shall coax them on to eat me up at once and not to hold off, as sometimes happens, through fear. And if they are reluctant, I shall force them to it.

This is brave talk, is it not? But, at the same time, it is the deepest truth of his life, the meaning of his life, which is the ineffaceable truth that it belongs not to him, but to Another, to Christ. What Ignatius is saying here is that, as von Balthasar so beautifully puts it, "there is one who, anticipating my existence, has suffered a martyrdom completely different from any that I or anyone else—even if he were Socrates—can suffer: a martyrdom for me, for my sake, vicariously for me who should have suffered it."

What precisely sets Christianity apart from every competing creed in the cosmos is that human life is based on, anchored to, the death of Another; rooted, therefore, in God's own death, which He freely enacted in the human being Jesus, the incarnate Word Himself, pierced and crucified for our sins. "The Christian is indebted to Another," says von Balthasar, and giving him the last word, he asks:

> And how else can he seriously acknowledge this debt than by following the same path as his Lord, since he has been very expressly invited to such discipleship and been just told in advance that the same thing will happen to the servant as to his master and to the pupil as to his teacher? This is the distinctive, special characteristic of the Christian martyr: he is "crucified with Christ," and the giving up of his life is an act of proper response, of self-evident gratitude. He does not die for an idea,

> even for the highest—not for human dignity, freedom or solidarity with the oppressed (although all these may be included and play a role). He dies with someone who has died for him in advance.

And so it is to Rome that Ignatius must go.

Chapter 13

From Judaism to Jesus

❧

WITH HIS LETTER TO the Church in Philadelphia—written in the wake of St. Ignatius and his guard leaving Smyrna for Troas, from which seaport the last of the letters will be sent before setting sail across the Adriatic to Neapolis, and then onto Rome—the vexed question of Judaism within the household of faith comes up in a more direct and detailed way than anything written heretofore. This grave issue threatens the unity and integrity of the Church in the most serious and unprecedented way. And unless it can be disarmed and thrown over, the threat posed by those Church members who have allowed themselves to be persuaded by it, the heart of the Catholic Thing will have been gutted. Nothing distinctively Christian will remain.

So, what's the real issue here? Why the insistence that, "if anyone preaches Judaism to you [i.e., the Church in

Philadelphia], pay no attention to him"? Or that those who persist in doing so, who refuse "to talk about Jesus Christ," are no better than "tombstones and graves of the dead, on which only human names are inscribed"? Why the urgency about fleeing at once such "wicked tricks and snares of the prince of this world," as represented by the Judaizers in their midst?

Leaving aside the colorful images about "specious wolves" and such, "who, by means of wicked pleasures, capture those who run God's race," how does Ignatius see the threat? Is there what one might call a "big sky" approach—some all-inclusive vision at work, whereby Ignatius seeks to arrest the faithful of Philadelphia? There is, indeed, and it is framed in the most sweeping way. Not on the strength of invective alone, although such passages contain some of the purest and most satisfying polemic, but rather by an appeal to the sheer comprehensive sweep of the Catholic Thing itself. For Ignatius, it radiates from the very center of the Church's Faith, rooted in the absolute primacy of Jesus Christ Himself. Thanks to whose divine and eternal status, humankind may be delivered from sin and death.

The argument, cast at the level of what Dr. Johnson calls "the grandeur of generality," thus moves, not from circumstance alone, but from definition, from which height the view becomes nothing less than all-encompassing.

"I urge you," it begins, "do not do things in cliques, but act as Christ's disciples." Then, poised to take off into the wild blue yonder, we see the outline of a vision so sublime that only Christology can make sense of it. But first a telling exchange occurs between Ignatius and the Judaizers, for whom Christianity will always remain a bridge too far. "When I heard some people saying [he means the Judaizers], 'If I don't find it in the original documents, I don't believe it in the gospel.'" What they mean, of course, is that only the Old Testament may provide the surest touchstone to belief, that the Law and the Prophets alone are the court of final appeal. If the truths of faith cannot be seen through that narrow and exclusive prism, which for them constitutes "the original documents," then there is no sense looking elsewhere. Christ cannot, therefore, be of any use to the children of God.

Ignatius will have none of it:

> I answered them, "But it is written there." They retorted, "That's just the question." To my mind it is Jesus Christ who is the original

> documents. The inviolable archives are his cross and death and his resurrection and the faith that came by him. It is by these things and through your prayers that I want to be justified.

What can this mean? It means that, finally, Revelation is an Event, the Second Person of the Blessed Trinity, coming down among us in the most daring possible descent, precisely in order, as the Scriptures say, "to pitch his tent in our very midst" (see John 1:14). Thus, in the most radical and profound way, Christianity remains utterly and forever unlike Judaism and, indeed, infinitely superior to it.

For Christians, God is "Emmanuel"—always and intimately among us. "Priests are a fine thing," writes Ignatius,

> but better still is the High Priest who was entrusted with the Holy of Holies. He alone was entrusted with God's secrets. He is the door to the Father. Through it there enter Abraham, Isaac, and Jacob, the prophets and apostles and the Church. All these find their place in God's unity. But there is something special

> about the gospel—I mean the coming of the Savior, our Lord Jesus Christ, his Passion and resurrection. The beloved prophets announced his coming; but the gospel is the crowning achievement forever.

What, then, are we to make of Judaism? Or of those Christians who will not let go of it, remaining fossilized within it, who cling to it as if salvation had never come at all? They must leave it all behind. And yet, by letting go of the one in order to find life and liberation in the other, they may be startled to discover that the fulfillment which they had long sought was there from the beginning, like the flower mysteriously present in the seed. The prophets knew this, of course, which is why Ignatius enjoins us to love them, "because they anticipated the gospel in their preaching and hoped for and awaited Him, and were saved by believing in him."

Christ Himself, he tells the Christians of Philadelphia, and those Judaizers willing to listen, "vouched for them and [thus] they form a real part of the gospel of our common hope."

Here the echo of Paul's magnificent Letter to the Romans, with its dazzling, unheard-of promise to the

People of the Book, can be heard resounding through Ignatius's own letter. Speaking to the Gentiles for whom he is God's appointed apostle, he longs to awaken the jealousy of his own race, "and thus save some of them. For if their rejection means the reconciliation of the world, what will their acceptance mean but life from the dead? If the dough offered as first fruits is holy, so is the whole lump; and if the root is holy, so are the branches" (Rom. 11:14–16).

But we Gentiles must not boast when recalling our many blessings. However, if we were inclined to boast, which is only natural, says St. Paul, "remember it is not you who support the root, but the root that supports you" (Rom. 11:18). In other words, God has not rejected His People, nor will He ever reject them. "For the gifts and the call of God are irrevocable" (Rom. 11:29).

Although strange that God chose a Jew in Paul to preach to the Gentiles, it was still odder that this same God Himself became a Jew. Without, to be sure, ceasing to be God. Thus did God use the Jewishness of Jesus to save the world. "Spiritually," Pope Pius XI would say, "we are all Semites."

Ignatius would be the first to agree.

Chapter 14

Facing the Peril of Docetism

❧

THERE ARE TWO OPPOSITE, yet equally erroneous views about Christ that Ignatius will need to confront directly in his correspondence with the churches of Asia and Rome—that of Docetism and Judaism. Of the two, Docetism poses the more significant danger. In fact, in his Letter to the Smyrnaeans, which is the penultimate installment in the series, he advises complete avoidance. A total boycott. So odious are its adherents, he insists to the Smyrnaeans, that they must never mention their names. Pray for their conversion, yes, but have nothing to do with them.

Why is that? One would think Judaism's denial of Christ's divinity a far graver affront to God than Docetism's disdain for His humanity. But for Ignatius, everything is personal, with all at stake in the struggle against Docetism. That is because, if God had never really become fully human, that he only appeared to assume mortal flesh as Docetism declares, then why bother traveling miles to die in Rome? To suffer hideously at the hands of wild beasts in the arena?

> If what our Lord did is a sham, so is my being in chains. Why, then, have I given myself up completely to death, fire, sword, and wild beasts?... What good does anyone do by praising me and then reviling my Lord by refusing to acknowledge that he carried around live flesh? He who denies this has completely disavowed him and carries a corpse around.

At the heart of Docetism is horror at the prospect of God—a purely spiritual being, untouched by the material world in any way—becoming one of us. From such defilement Docetism instinctively recoils, seeing it as a grotesquerie of which nothing more revolting can be imagined. For there is nothing more alien to such heretics than the claim, the sheer shocking belief that the Absolute and Transcendent God Himself should condescend to enter the material world as a little child—from zygote to infant—in order to rescue and redeem a fallen world.

"What sets Christianity apart from other religions," writes von Balthasar in an essay on "The Incarnation of God,"

> is the offensive claim that the one who bears all names and is yet without name, who as the Scripture says "is everything" (Sir 43:27), has once and for all declared himself identical with a tiny something or someone in the vast cosmos and among the countless millions of swarming humanity—identical with someone who can make such monstrously exclusive statements about himself as "I am the door … all who have come before me are thieves and robbers" (Jn 10:7f) and "No one knows the Father but the Son and him to whom the Son will reveal it" (Mt 11:27).

What is Docetism's response? How does it cope with the messy details of Christ's own death, for instance, an event so obviously and undeniably real that not a single creedal confession fails to record it as having taken place at a most particular time and place? Indeed, in every reference to this most climactic moment of Christ's life, when He chooses to depart from this world, it is always "under Pontius Pilate"—again, a perfectly real and historically verifiable figure—that Christ will suffer, die, and be buried. And, then, of course, rise triumphant on the third day. Only an imbecile, or a crazed idealogue, would doubt this historical fact.

How, then, do they respond? Faced with this pesky little detail at the center of the story? Ah, but these are devilishly clever heretics, for whom even the plainest of facts must never be allowed to get in the way of a narrative steeped in hatred and fantasy. Christ's Passion and death? Not a problem. Just substitute Simon of Cyrene at the eleventh hour and—poof!—it all goes away. Nothing untoward has happened. Not a trace of the unseemly will be permitted to spoil the story. And, certainly, no mere mortal will ever be in a position, as it were, to dagger God to death.

So, will the good people of Smyrna buy it? Not if Ignatius has any say in the matter. And he has heaps to say to the Church of Smyrna, the very place, after all, from which the first four of his letters were sent. "You are a wonderful credit to God and real saints," he tells them.

> Who, as regards our Blessed Lord, are absolutely convinced that on the human side he was

> actually sprung from David's line, Son of God according to God's will and power, actually born of a virgin, baptized by John, that "all righteousness might be fulfilled in him" (Mat 3:15), and actually crucified for us in the flesh, under Pontius Pilate and Herod the Tetrarch.

In other words, nothing was feigned. In the agony and abandonment of the Cross, the pain and the loss were real. Not only was there no masquerading the misery, no affectation amid the afflictions, but it was all done for us. Here, in two tiny words—*pro nobis*—which the Church early on inserted into the Creed, are contained the deepest reason for hope we have.

> For it was for our sakes that he suffered all this, to save us. And he genuinely suffered, as even he genuinely raised himself. It is not as some unbelievers say, that his Passion was a sham. It's they who are a sham! Yes, and their fate will fit their fancies—they will be ghosts and apparitions.

Ignatius warns the Church in Smyrna against being misled by Docetism, lest they fall into the same heresy. So vast are its tentacles, he adds, that even the cosmos itself is not immune to its evil reach. "Heavenly beings, the splendor of angels, principalities, visible and invisible, if they fail to believe in Christ's blood, they too are doomed." What it all comes down to is the Holy Eucharist, the scandalous particularity of which will always remain a barrier to the enemies of faith.

This is precisely why, Ignatius reminds us, they shun the Sacrifice of the Altar. "They hold aloof from the Eucharist and from services of prayer, because they refuse to admit that the Eucharist is the flesh of our Savior Jesus Christ." If only they were, he says, "to pay attention to the prophets and above all to the gospel," for it is only there that "we get a clear picture of the Passion and see that the resurrection has really happened."

His final warhead thus launched, Ignatius has little left to say. Save only the following theological zinger, which concerns a single phrase never before uttered in the history of Christianity, to wit, the Catholic Church. Long and hallowed usage has turned it into a standard canonical commonplace instantly understood by the faithful everywhere. It appears at the very end of a sentence in which Ignatius, having first urged the faithful "to flee from schism as the source of mischief and to follow the bishop as Jesus Christ did the Father," concludes as follows: "Where the bishop is present, there let the congregation gather, just as where Jesus Christ is, there is the Catholic Church."

A fitting end, it would seem, to a perfect letter.

Chapter 15

The Final Letter

TAKEN TO TROAS, A port city located along the northern route through Asia Minor to the Aegean Sea — across which lies Europe and the final, fateful leg of the journey to Rome — St. Ignatius of Antioch will write three letters. His last letter will be sent to the saintly bishop of Smyrna, Polycarp, numbered among the immortals of the early Church. Like Ignatius, Polycarp will wear the laurels of martyrdom, the crowing jewel of his old age.

But not yet. In fact, not until nearly a half century later when, as a very old man about to be burned at the stake, he will boldly announce his faith before the whole crowd of unbelieving pagans and Jews. "Take the oath," shouts the proconsul, "and I shall release you! Curse Christ!" To all of which the aged Polycarp will calmly reply, "Eighty-six years I have served him, and he never did me any wrong. How can I blaspheme my King who saved me?" Whereupon the fagots are gathered, the fire is lit, which at once assumes the shape of a vaulted chamber, "like a ship's sail filled by the wind," eyewitnesses report, "making a wall around the body of the martyr." And, behold, there he will stand before the astonished crowd, "not as burning flesh, but as bread baking or as gold and silver refined in a furnace. And we perceived such a sweet aroma as the breath of incense or some other precious spice."

To add to the amazement, Polycarp's body does not burn. As a result, the proconsul orders one of his executioners to dispatch him with a dagger.

> And when he did this a dove and a great quantity of blood came forth, so that the fire was quenched and the whole crowd marveled that there should be such a difference between the unbelievers and the elect.

Ignatius's hasty letter to Polycarp ought to come as a surprise to us given Polycarp's credentials.

Can there really be anything touching on matters of either faith or morals about which Polycarp does not already know everything? What more does a man who first heard the good news as a child from the Beloved Apostle himself, St. John the Divine, require? Who, years later, while visiting Rome to confer with the pope, will run into the heretic Marcion—who, having just eviscerated the entire Old Testament owing to the fact that the God of Jesus Christ could not have been its author—and when asked whether Polycarp knew him, will straightaway be told, "Yes, I know that you are the firstborn of Satan!"

So learned and brave a witness to Christ would seem quite competent enough to manage his own affairs. But, then, of course, Ignatius's Letter to Polycarp—the very last, and the shortest, of the seven written and sent since his arrest in Antioch—sheds no new light. "It is because I am well aware of your earnest sincerity," he assures him, "that I limit my appeal to so few words." And such words as he may feel it necessary to pass along are intended rather to remind Polycarp of things he is not likely ever to have forgotten anyway. Not if he is to stay strong for an end that will surely prove as bloody as the one Ignatius himself awaits.

> Just as pilots demand winds and a storm-tossed sailor a harbor, so times like these demand a person like you. With your help we

> will both get to God. . . . The prize, as you very well know, is immortality and eternal life.

Gratitude permeates Ignatius's last letter to Polycarp, the result of having known the man whose very name *Polycarp* means "much fruit." In Polycarp, the face of Christ is made visible. And while the young Polycarp had his own encounter with Christ through John, whose face was filled with light whenever he spoke of seeing Jesus for the first time, so too will Ignatius espy the same face upon the countenance of Polycarp.

"While I was impressed," he tells him, "with your godly mind, which is fixed, as it were, on an immovable rock, I am more than grateful that I was granted the sight of your holy face. God grant I may never forget it!"

Let us steel ourselves, he seems to be saying to his episcopal friend, for the fearful ordeal that is to come, an ordeal that will only end in death. And so, in exhorting Polycarp to play the man, he does not wish to detach himself from the same performance. Let us together, therefore, stand our ground, "like an anvil under the hammer," resolutely receiving blow upon blow. "A great athlete," he declares, "must suffer blows to conquer. And especially for God's sake must we put up with everything, so that he will put up with us."

Like a runner who keeps his eyes always focused on the finish line, so also must the Christian keep his eyes fixed upon Heaven. That is because, as von Balthasar reminds us in his *Short Primer for Unsettled Laymen*, "the light of Christ," to which all that we say and do must point, "proves itself and thus repels what is false; it is *index sui et falsi*. Thus everything depends upon whether the light of Christ in its incomparable unity becomes evident."

What is finally at stake here is nothing less than "the still point of the turning world," that mystic point where all things come together in Christ. It is Christ, you see, who furnishes the *kairos*, the Now Moment, which is that divinely appointed hour of divine-human intersection, where history and mystery, nature and grace, the carnal and the celestial are joined together in a common dance.

And while the usual, customary curiosity of most men "searches past and future / And clings to that dimension," the would-be saint must look elsewhere, must bend every muscle, as it were, "to apprehend the point of intersection of the timeless with time." T. S. Eliot further says that there

> is an occupation for the saint—
> No occupation either, but something given

> And taken, in a lifetime's death in love,
> Ardour and selflessness and self-surrender.

Alas, for most of us, continues Eliot, "there is only the unattended / Moment, the moment in and out of time, / The distraction fit, lost in a shaft of sunlight." So many "hints and guesses," continues Eliot,

> Hints followed by guesses; and the rest
> Is prayer, observance, discipline, thought and
> action.
> The hint half-guessed, the gift half under-
> stood, is Incarnation.
> Here the impossible union
> Of spheres of existence is actual,
> Here the past and future
> Are conquered, and reconciled.

And so Ignatius tells Polycarp to be ever vigilant for the promised appearance of God, who breaks into our world with the surprise and spontaneity of a child, both sudden and unforeseen, yet longed for from the beginning. And, of course, He never disappoints.

> Mark the times. Be on the alert for him who is above time, the Timeless, the Unseen, the One who became visible for our sakes, who was beyond touch and passion, yet for our sakes became subject to suffering, and endured everything for us.

Ignatius makes one final point, which communicates a sense of wonderment. "News has reached me," he tells Polycarp, "that, thanks to your prayers, the Church at Antioch in Syria is now at peace. At this I have taken new courage and, relying on God, I have set my mind at rest—assuming, that is, I may get to God through suffering, and at the resurrection prove to be your disciple." And so his last request is that his friend write at once to the various churches of Asia, importuning them to give all glory and honor and thanksgiving to God for so blessed and unexpected a deliverance. For here is Ignatius's very own Church, the See of Antioch, the place from which he'd been so cruelly torn away by the emperor Trajan for the mob's amusement in Rome. Free at last from the grip of a persecution of which he, Ignatius, had been so conspicuous—and celebrated—an example.

Epilogue on St. Ignatius

❧

When the last line is written about St. Ignatius, leaving little more to be said about the letters he wrote, the life he lived—what should the reader take away from his story? Is there anything especially endearing to pass along, an insight to remember him best? A certain quality of mind and heart, perhaps, to account for so great an admiration and reverence felt by the Church for this extraordinary figure from the early second century?

In his preparation for death, Ignatius evinced the most perfect imitation of Jesus Christ that is possible for any man to give. Christ became the answer to the question that was his life, that the whole meaning of his being began and ended with Him and in Him. Like all the saints before and after, Ignatius not only knew where the key was to open the Kingdom, but owned it as well, whereby all the riches of Heaven were handed over to him.

Christians have always held the martyrs in the highest esteem precisely for believing and acting as heirs to the Kingdom of Heaven. As von Balthasar puts it in his essay on "Martyrdom and Mission": They were able to solve the riddle put to all and win the prize.... They knew the password.

And the password was Jesus Christ. For Him alone they wished to lay down everything.

> What the early Christians loved and admired about their martyrs was this: that in giving their lives they were able to give a full, somehow humanly possible, adequate response to the deed of their Lord, who as the consubstantial Son of God possessed the competency and the power to deliver himself up for all, thus revealing the depths of the Father's heart, the sentiments of the divine origin.

This was no headlong escape from the world, no flight from life owing to craven fear and neurosis. But the passion of a bishop and martyr who has fallen head over heels in love with God, and who longs above all to cleave to the One he loves.

"One should not rush into martyrdom," warns von Balthasar, "for who knows what one still has to do for God in this life? But, equally, one may not refuse it when it is inevitably demanded." It is not possible, in other words, to so etherealize the idea of following Christ that one never has to behave as though one were actually following Him at all. Christianity is not an idea one has become somehow enamored of; it is a Person—concretely, scandalously even, incarnate in a human being named Jesus—to whom one is wholly and intimately joined. And what else does it mean to be a disciple if not to follow the Master all the way to the Cross? Where else is He going if not to Golgotha? As von Balthasar declares,

> Why otherwise would Jesus have invited his friends to follow him so closely and foretold for them persecution, rejection, court trials, even crucifixion (Jn 21)? This close bond between the follower and the "founder of our faith" (Heb 12:2) was fully familiar to the early Church.

Here, then, is the nub of the matter, the hinge on which the door of every bloody martyrdom opens and shuts. It is precisely, as von Balthasar says,

> this mysterious parity — notwithstanding the disparity — between Christ and his Church, the Redeemer and those redeemed by him. The reasons for breaking down when faced with martyrdom may have been fear and cowardice, but not doubts about the truth of the faith.

And Ignatius, like most members of the Church annealed by baptism into the mysteries of Christ, had no doubts about the truth of our common Faith. Unlike many Christians, however, he courageously chose to die for Christ when his faith was put to the ultimate test. His seven letters are a testament to his great sanctity, for he practiced what he preached by laying down his life for his flock.

St. Ignatius, bishop and martyr, pray for us!

About the Author

Dr. Regis Martin is a professor of systematic theology at Franciscan University of Steubenville, specializing in courses on the Trinity, church, grace, sacraments, the Apostolic Fathers, and the world of the Catholic Literary Revival. He is a regular EWTN panelist on *Franciscan University Presents*. He received his STD magna cum laude from the Pontifical University of St. Thomas (Angelicum) in Rome in 1988. He is the author of a number of books, including, most recently, *Looking for Lazarus: A Preview of the Resurrection*. He is married and the father of ten children.

Sophia Institute

Sophia Institute is a nonprofit institution that seeks to nurture the spiritual, moral, and cultural life of souls and to spread the gospel of Christ in conformity with the authentic teachings of the Roman Catholic Church.

Sophia Institute Press fulfills this mission by offering translations, reprints, and new publications that afford readers a rich source of the enduring wisdom of mankind.

Sophia Institute also operates the popular online resource CatholicExchange.com. *Catholic Exchange* provides world news from a Catholic perspective as well as daily devotionals and articles that will help readers to grow in holiness and live a life consistent with the teachings of the Church.

In 2013, Sophia Institute launched Sophia Institute for Teachers to renew and rebuild Catholic culture through service to Catholic education. With the goal of nurturing the spiritual, moral, and cultural life of souls, and an abiding respect for the role and work of teachers, we strive to provide materials and programs that are at once enlightening to the mind and ennobling to the heart; faithful and complete, as well as useful and practical.

Sophia Institute gratefully recognizes the Solidarity Association for preserving and encouraging the growth of our apostolate over the course of many years. Without their generous and timely support, this book would not be in your hands.

www.SophiaInstitute.com
www.CatholicExchange.com
www.SophiaTeachers.org